AUTHORED BY

What got you here, won't get you there...

YOUR CAREER
2.0®

A Survival Guide for
The Battered Career®
and Investor Syndrome®

DEDICATION

We dedicate this book to the tens of thousands of clients who have allowed us to guide them through their Journey of Discovery. Courageous people who have made their dreams come true by taking the path less traveled. You inspire us every day. May you, the reader, also achieve your dreams and may this book empower you and assist you in your journey.

The Entrepreneur's Source Dream Team

TABLE OF CONTENTS

INTRODUCTION

(From unEmployment to Empowerment®)

Chances are that you are reading this book because you are among the 75% of the population that is seeking self-sufficiency. Most likely you have a desire to find a better way and to improve your current situation. Perhaps you are tired of being a victim of the Battered Career Syndrome® or the Battered Investor Syndrome® which keep people going back to hopeless situations with the expectation that this time around they will be different–that the job and the stock markets will go back to the heydays enjoyed in years past.

In all probability you are painfully aware that the job market has changed dramatically in the last 25 years with more and more layoffs every time there is a downward shift in the economy, with jobs being lost to cheaper labor in other countries and entire industries moving overseas. We have been living in the Career Revolution era where job security no longer exists and pension plans are a thing of the past. Our families, our income, our emotional wellbeing, and the way we must plan for the future have all been drastically affected.

Maybe there have been cutbacks in your company. Maybe you have been lucky enough to have survived them but wonder when your turn is coming. Or maybe you didn't survive the latest layoff and are currently unemployed or underemployed, or perhaps you have even joined the un-employable ranks. Increased levels of fears and uncertainty in today's workplace don't leave much room for inspiration or empowerment. In fact, when was the last time you felt inspired or empowered? Think back to when you were a child and the possibilities were endless. You felt you could do anything. You felt empowered, right? You could dare to dream because failure was not even an option. You had the ability to focus on the end goal and not on the obstacles in your way. It's time to regain that ability and redefine your goals. Where is your professional future headed? Are you on track? Will your current path take you where you want to go?

This book is the starting point of your journey towards self-sufficiency and financial freedom. Together we will build the framework to define your goals, needs, and ex-pectations, and assist you in determining the proper vehicle to help you attain them. We will explore where the Career Revolution may have taken you and how you can break free from the corporate world. We will also point out some of the traps that may hold you back from getting the Income, Lifestyle, Wealth and Equity you desire. And, we will give you the platform whereby you can build your own success story and create a new, improved version of yourself—YOU

2.0®. We will show you how to explore your options with an adventurer's mindset. Yet, we'll create the space you need to feel safe. Through a coaching experience, you will find that you can embark on a Journey of Discovery with The Entrepreneur's Source Dream Team as your guide to support you as you make your dreams come true.

It is all part of the voyage from *unEmployment to Empowerment*®.

Are you ready?

CHAPTER 1: THE CAREER REVOLUTION

Over the last 25 years, the job market has changed drastically, affecting our families, our careers, and the way we live our lives and plan our futures. Today's job market is certainly nothing like what our parents and grandparents experienced. Back then most people worked for the same company for 30 or 40 years and could count on the security of a paycheck, benefits, and a pension plan that afforded them a similar standard of living to what they had prior to retirement. This reality no longer exists. It's a thing of the past—a distant memory of the way things used to be.

The Career Revolution has meant the loss of job security. Pension plans we used to count on for our golden years have been replaced by hard-to-fund self-directed retirement accounts. Layoffs have become the norm every time there is a downward shift in the economy. Jobs are disappearing as a result of technological advancements or going to cheaper labor in other countries, and entire industries moving overseas have become the new normal. Nowadays the "Made in America" label is so rare that many of us have to ponder the last time we saw it. For most people, today's jobs are just that—a job that covers the very basic necessities. Having a job no longer implies having a career that can lead to Income, Lifestyle, Wealth, and Equity (I.L.W.E.®). Instead, for many, their jobs have become merely the means to survive and pay bills. What does JOB stand for? For many it means: Just Over Broke. All of these changes have created a movement from job security to job insecurity.

In the past, people based their career decisions, education, commitments, and goals on an abiding sense of job security—an assumption that has since been proven false by the corporate world. Greater numbers of layoffs thinning the workforce and corporate giants buckling are the signatures of the current job market. Today there are unique market issues that threaten peoples' stability. Savings are down, home equity for some has disappeared, and stress has never been higher.

Many people from the baby boomer generation have been displaced and are concerned about their futures. They worry that they may not get their jobs back, or that the jobs may not come back at the income level they need or want. Real income is deteriorating at a rapid rate.

At the other end of the spectrum, young employees are entering a market unlike anything that existed before. The young people who are entering the workforce today may have more than 10 different jobs before they retire and, for the majority, these changes are brought about by external circumstance and not by their own choosing.

To add to the sense of unpredictability and lack of control of today's employees, regardless of their age, the loss of the equity in their homes, and the diminished value of their stock can make the future look very bleak and create extreme levels of stress. Dealing with uncertainty can throw people into a victim position or it can propel them into a more empowered path. Being proactive in your career and with your investments puts you on the empowered path.

Not all is gloom and doom. It's true that the Career Revolution means that we live in an uncertain world where job security doesn't exist any longer. Yet, it's important that you realize this: *You may have lost your job, but that doesn't mean you have lost your career or that you are powerless.* It certainly may feel that way from time to time, but you have choices that can empower you. You need to consider that what traditionally may have been regarded as too risky, such as business ownership for example, may be the less risky option in today's economy.

You owe it to yourself, and to your family, to explore the options associated with becoming self-sufficient. If you equip yourself with knowledge and information, and apply yourself in a way you have never done before, the Career Revolution might truly revolutionize your life. Everything you have done up until this point in your life, in essence, can be considered research and development, You 1.0. Are you ready for the next version of you? YOU 2.0®? Reading this book is your first step.

Let's first explore the realities of the Career Revolution.

Battered Career Syndrome®/Battered Investor Syndrome®

Have you ever been in a situation that has not made you happy, and while you've acknowledged that fact, you weren't able to see any options for escaping? Perhaps you admitted to the problem but put off trying to fix it, or thought that if you gave it another chance the next time would be different–the situation would change? Sometimes the simple act of recognizing that things are not going well, and seeing beyond the illusion, is a comfort in and of itself—a way to feel that progress has been made, even though the situation has not been rectified.

For example, in the "new normal" that we are currently experiencing, we may be less likely to fall back on the illusion of security and more willing to admit being duped by corporate dependency. While some people hold out hope that the economy might one day return to the traditional model, not too many are counting on that. Most people understand that things have changed, yet their behavior patterns, which are based on habits they developed through years of working within the corporate system, are still on autopilot. They know there is a problem, but they are too habituated or fearful to extract themselves from the situation.

This employee mindset bears some resemblance to that of a battered spouse. Being involved in an abusive relationship is obviously a very serious situation; and in no way are we making light of it. The fact is, however, that there are a number of parallels between abused and abuser, and most employees and their traditional employers.

It's a common occurrence for employees to admit that something is wrong while remaining caught in the cycle of behavior that is keeping them entangled. It's not a conscious choice but simply the state of affairs to which they have become accustomed. Seeing their friends get fired, getting double the workload for less pay, and watching as their benefits are whittled away have become the status quo. They don't believe there is an alternative, so they stick with it even as the situation deteriorates. They are suffering from what we call the Battered Career Syndrome®.

Take Paul, for example, a sales executive who has spent his entire career within the structure of the traditional job mold. With education and experience that have allowed him to climb the ranks to the executive suite, he has spent his working life putting in long hours, traveling for weeks on end, and missing out on time with his family and friends. He honestly believes he has to put up with these conditions to procure steady income.

Now that Paul has reached the executive level, he continues to deal with his unsatisfying job in hopes that things will improve, or at least result in a better paycheck. Each day he returns to work, anticipating that things will be better, only to find that he is repeating the cycle over and over again. He is going nowhere and doesn't have the first clue about how to escape the situation. The most likely alternative—self-employment—seems too frightening, and he has no idea what other options might be out there. Paul is a classic example of Battered Career Syndrome®.

Such an employee is much like a battered spouse who is too scared to leave because he or she has no idea what the future might hold and no plan for facing it. Employees trapped by Battered Career Syndrome® continue in the same cycle because they believe there will be a paycheck, even if they don't have an ideal work environment. They believe there is no alternative and that, if they stay, things somehow will get better.

It's only when the urge to protect themselves and their families overcomes their fear that they finally venture beyond the traditional employee mindset. Their life-changing moment comes when they take that first step and do something they've never done before, and then find it is not nearly as frightening as the situation they left.

So much has happened in the business environment during recent years that most of us are walking around in a daze, feeling beaten and uncertain about what just happened. There aren't many people who have escaped the Battered Career Syndrome® or, for that matter, the Battered Investors Syndrome® that takes people back to reactive investments even after losing almost everything with the fluctuations of the stock market. As a result, most of us continue to exist in a cycle of insanity—*repeating the same actions but expecting different results.* For that to change, a fundamental shift must take place in the way we think about our careers and about our investments. It's time for a wake-up call!

The Trade-Off

A by-product of the Career Revolution has been the tremendous number of trade-offs employees have been forced to make in order to keep their jobs. Have you ever spent too much time commuting or traveling? Have you had to relocate from one city to the next just to keep up with the rat race that your job has become? Have you felt guilty about missing too many of your children's recitals or baseball games, or regretted not spending enough time with your family?

In today's financial environment, it has become nearly impossible to earn an income, maintain a lifestyle, and build a nest egg without sacrificing nearly all of your time to the job. With approximately 77 percent of Americans now living paycheck to paycheck (a statistic that is increasing each year), it is painfully clear that few workers have the time or money to do anything other than survive. People are now taking jobs averaging 23 percent less income, while having to expend nearly 32 percent more time, energy, and effort.1 American parents spend 40 percent less time with their children today than they did in 1965.2 You trade off time with your children and spouse for the security of a steady paycheck, but that security no longer exists.

Time with your family is not the only trade-off you are making. You are also foregoing the opportunity to follow your dreams. Today, people often work 50, 60, or even 70 hours a week just to keep up. That's time and energy spent building someone else's dream and contributing to their Income, Lifestyle, Wealth and Equity—not yours, or your family's.

In fact, Lawrence Johnson, Chief Economist for the International Labor Organization, said: *"Workers in the United States are putting in more hours than anyone else in the industrialized world."*3 Why? Unfortunately, it is usually to build someone else's wealth. Whether we want to admit it or not, that's essentially what most employees are doing today.

This realization can create a lot of frustration. But just for a moment, set all that frustration aside and imagine a different future. What would happen if you started spending all those hours doing something for yourself? What would your life look like? What would you do if failure were not an option? When you ask yourself these questions, you reach a point at which you begin to see possibilities and *frustration turns into fascination.*

Turning Sand Into Pearls

How do you turn that growing awareness of other possibilities into a tangible goal? Our research shows that 75 percent of all adults are searching for something other than a job. They are seeking self-sufficiency and financial independence and they are experiencing constant frustration. They have a sense that there is something better out there, a different path from the rat race.

Think of your increasing dissatisfaction with the traditional job market as a grain of sand inside an oyster. It is a persistent irritation; however, that is not necessarily a bad thing. When properly channeled, that grain of sand eventually develops into a precious pearl. In terms of your career, this constant irritation produced by the frustration about the job market motivates you to look outside of what you know and allows you to see greater possibilities for your future.

The truth is that the economy and the job market are never going to be what they once were—not in our lifetime, and not in our children's lifetime. We have entered a completely different world, and looking the other way and denying the reality of the situation is no longer an option. Acknowledging these facts is the catalyst for change. It galvanizes you to turn your grain of sand into a pearl.

Possibilities, Options, and Dreams

By now you might be asking yourself if there is any bright spot in all of this seemingly hopeless reality. The answer is a resounding, "YES!" Your next step begins with your Possibilities, Options, and Dreams. They all exist, and they are within your grasp. To create the empowerment needed to reach them, you must first transform your mindset.

Think of it like maintaining a healthy weight. Everybody knows the solutions, yet empowering someone to change the way they eat and exercise is a different issue altogether. Giving up on the desired result in the short term is almost always easier than developing the habits that will ultimately result in what people say they want. In the same way, you know you need to alter the way you look at your career and the road to greater Income, Lifestyle, Wealth, and Equity to achieve what you desire. Now you simply have to find the right tools and follow through on your goals. This may sound easier said than done. Motivational speaker Brian Klemmer once said, *"If how-to's were enough, we would all be skinny, rich, and happy,"* suggesting that we need something else to increase the likelihood of success. People who work with a nutritionist or a physical trainer are more likely to achieve their desired weight or fitness goals. The same is true for those who work with a career or business coach.

Since we know that the old options are unreliable, the question is this: *How will you take control of your financial*

future to get from where you are to where you want to be? This
may be a major transition for you, and fear of the unknown
can be a powerful obstacle, even when you know you are
moving toward something better—in the end, something
more secure and more under your control.

Making the Switch

The traditional corporate job has always required a
time-and-effort based mindset. To even contemplate the
possibility of focusing on the results of self-sufficiency that
come with self-employment can be a difficult and scary
transition.

Historically most employees could exist in a time-and-effort economy whether or not they produced results. Business owners, however, have always depended solely on their
results. This can be a crippling revelation. Very possibly,
for the first time, everything that people would normally
depend on has vanished. The leadership, relationships, and
opportunities they always turned to are suddenly no longer
the infrastructure to support them.

It helps to remember that the corporate world has been
proven unreliable. Education and experience no longer
ensure a secure job, and the stock market fluctuates wildly,
even on the best of days. Yet, the most important thing
to keep in mind is that the formula that got you to your

current situation will not be the one that can help you reach your vision of a more prosperous future. Instead, you must look at winning formulas from your past—paths that may not have led to the perfect corporate job, but rather to other successes in your life—and use those as a basis for greater confidence in switching to more proactive career and investment vehicles.

Breaking Free of the Corporate World

How many of us would like to steer our own ships? Pretty much everyone, right? Yet, it's amazing how few of us actually do it. Perhaps it's because it requires a level of personal responsibility we are not used to facing. However, to leave behind what isn't working for us, we must embrace a results-oriented attitude. And, it all starts with gathering facts and information and exploring new territories. The biggest mistake most people make in working on their Income, Lifestyle, Wealth and Equity goals is failing to learn about the options they have to achieve them. Educating yourself requires taking personal responsibility for your future, and it's the ONLY way to discover what is possible.

The simplest, most direct route to controlling your own destiny and your financial future is by observing how others do it; and then, learning what your options are for doing the same. For most of us, taking control usually means starting our own business. And this option can be a scary one when we are still living in the past, when having a job was the less risky path. Therefore, most people tend to immediately dismiss business ownership as an option.

There are many reasons why people don't take that leap to business ownership. In our experience, however, the main reason is that they don't know where to start. They are terrified of striking out into the unknown all by themselves. And, unfortunately for some, the fear of failure is stronger than their desire for success. The final excuse is usually a paralyzing combination of these reasons. Don't fall into that trap. Don't let fear win. At the very least, you owe it to yourself and to your family to explore what's possible.

If you find yourself jumping to conclusions right now, thinking, *"Okay, I know what this is about. This is never going to work for me,"* we urge you to make no hasty decisions. Don't limit your options. Keep an open mind. Be open to even scary possibilities, gather the information and do the research. Doing so will help you look at the facts instead of reacting to preconceived notions and emotions. Be willing to explore; we'll guide you through your Journey of Discovery. It's your way out; it will help you break free from the corporate chains. We are not asking you to make any decisions prematurely; in fact, we will not ask you to make any decisions at all. Once you gather the facts, you'll reach a point of clarity and the best next step will be evident.

Ninety-five percent of the people who have gone through this "Journey of Discovery" admittedly say that they ended up discovering options they would have never considered before or would have prematurely dismissed. We helped them not rush to conclusions prematurely. We reassured them that, if upon gathering the facts they validate that their first reaction was on target, then they have a new perspective with which they can go back to the job market. They will no longer feel that irritation they felt before because they have done their homework. We encourage you to do the same and to remain open to possibilities, and to be like a child for whom failure is not an option. Go ahead and explore the world of possibilities; they can lead you to your dreams. And, we'll start by helping you write your own success story—your YOU 2.0®

CHAPTER 2: WRITING YOUR OWN SUCCESS STORY
YOU 2.0®

What will real success look like for you?

Because success doesn't look the same for everyone, one of the most important objectives of your Journey of Discovery is to answer this question. Your response will be unique and will depend on many factors such as your age, dreams, personality, financial position, family obligations, and past experience. For example, baby boomer John is nearing retirement age and suddenly finds that his Social Security benefits won't go as far as he had expected. He is looking for something different than Beth, who is only at the midpoint of her career and finds she isn't happy with the rigid structure of her current corporate environment. On the other hand, Doug is in his late 20's and hoping to pay off his college loans, whereas 30-year-old Emily has two kids and wants to start saving for their college educations, while still having time to help them with their homework. All four of these people want greater Income, Lifestyle, Wealth, and Equity; however, the specifics of their goals for the future, their success stories, and the paths they take to get there will most likely differ dramatically.

Creating your own success story begins with shifting your paradigm so you can start to see yourself and your aspirations as the greatest proactive tool in your arsenal. Such a shift creates a multiplier effect, which allows you to get significantly greater results with less time, energy, and effort. Have you ever heard the saying, *"What got you here won't get you there"?* This aphorism is especially relevant to our career. We need to scrutinize our own personal actions. In other words, we must ask: *"Do we tend to take the path of least resistance and avoid looking at ourselves and take responsibility for our lives and futures? Do we close ourselves to possibilities just because we have never considered them before? Are we afraid of change?"*

A complete rethink of what "career" means is needed when we are writing our success stories in today's reality. Mankind has gone through the type of change that is necessary today many times before. Not to oversimplify a complex situation, but perhaps it helps to think about it in the following way: In the early days, in order to survive, there were hunters and gatherers. As mankind evolved, we started to farm on land. We created ways to harvest what we sowed with reasonable predictability. Then, came the Industrial Revolution and with it came the creation of jobs—the kind of jobs that many are now still hoping for today, where there is a vast dependency on the employer. And times have changed again; we have entered the Digital Revolution that along economic challenges and globalization ignited the Career Revolution. Today you may not be employed, or you may not have your ideal job and not even the slightest hope of getting it, but you still can have a career. The occupation that can allow you to achieve your desired Income, Lifestyle, Wealth, and Equity still exists, you just need an open mind to find it.

Our Journey of Discovery doesn't promise you anything. It simply holds up a mirror to help you see the life you want to live and then shines a light on the options that can help you achieve that life. When clients first come to us, they are looking for material things outside themselves—better opportunities, the perfect job, or the latest hot franchise opportunity. The purpose of this journey is to help you build the future you desire and define the Income, Lifestyle, Wealth, and Equity goals you're seeking.

A critical component of this journey is the safe space it provides for you to explore your options and to figure out what you want and what works best for you. After all, you're the only one who can define *your* success. We have created a learning journey to the often overwhelming task of redefining your mindset and career path, and this approach will empower you, no matter what decisions you end up making about your future.

It's easy to think that you don't deserve this safe space, or to play the tough person and think that you don't need it. Don't let your fear stand in the way of exploring your options in a truly safe environment. You don't have to jump off any cliffs, but simply look at the options with clearer eyes and a better sense of what is possible.

Income, Lifestyle, Wealth and Equity (I.L.W.E.®)

As you begin to define your goals, it helps to relate them to four basic concepts: "Income," "Lifestyle," "Wealth," and "Equity". We have used these terms previously as a way of pinpointing some tangible goals for the future, and they all are directly affected by your professional career. However, what exactly do they mean? Let us take a moment to define these four important terms as they'll help you determine what direction you want your future to take.

Income

Income is typically a shorter-term goal. You can see its effects immediately with larger regular influx of money and growing bank account balances. While this term seems fairly straightforward, in reality, our concept of income and what we want out of it has changed drastically. Where once the people who started on the Journey of Discovery wanted to double or even triple their incomes, now many are simply trying to maintain the same levels they made before. If they have lost their jobs, getting another one at the previous salary has become increasingly difficult as jobs are disappearing or they are being filled by younger employees willing to accept a smaller paycheck.

Most people became accustomed to having their career and incomes grow consistently between the ages of 35 and 50; but this is no longer so for most people. Income expectations are being upended, and many employees have come to realize that they traded off time with their family for a paycheck that no longer exists. As a result, goals revolving around income have become more about finding security outside the corporate world during a time when real income is declining, starting salaries are decreasing, and long-term unemployment for those 55 and older is growing exponentially.

Lifestyle

Lifestyle is another short-term goal with immediate visible effects. We hear our clients say they've been working 60-hour weeks and now want to earn a dependable living while being able to fully live their lives. They want the freedom and flexibility to attend their kids' soccer games or have romantic dinners with their spouses. In previous years, everything revolved around having a bigger income, and now their focus has shifted to having the same level of income outside the rat race in terms of the traditional workplace. These people are not afraid to work, and they know they still have to put in the hours; they just want to do it in a way that better molds their careers around their lifestyles.

The corporate world had most of us convinced that the only way to give our families a prosperous lifestyle was with trade-offs. Devoting yourself entirely to your job was supposed to guarantee that you would one day get that golden parachute. Unfortunately, for many, the golden parachute turned out to be a trap door.

Wealth

As we have seen, income comes first. Once you develop income, you create a lifestyle that suits you, and the right opportunity will allow you to do both. Income and lifestyle are immediate concerns; however, wealth centers more on the years to come. Wealth is about taking your increasing income and growing it even larger. You invest. You diversify. You purchase other assets that have wealth-building elements to them, and you save for the future.

Equity

The final piece of the puzzle is Equity, the strategy you develop once you have all your assets in place. Equity is your ownership in any asset after all debts associated with that asset are paid off. For example, a car or house with no outstanding debt is considered the owner's equity because he or she can readily sell the item for cash. Stocks are equity because they represent ownership in a corporation. When you choose owning a business as your way to self-sufficiency and financial independence, you would be building equity as you pay off the debts associated with the business.

Taking Control of Your Life

The problem we encounter today is that many people no longer believe that wealth and equity can grow in today's world. Back in the heyday of corporations, people spent a great deal of time thinking about these things; now that the reset button has been hit, all bets are off. As a result, many believe they must jettison their expectations and settle for less today and in the future; and, unfortunately, that's the example they're setting for their children. Young people are witnessing the struggle and heartbreak their parents go through in the traditional job system. We owe our children to show them that there is a better way; we need to show them how to be ready to change and to adapt when the situation requires it—most importantly, we need to be an example of how to be open to different possibilities.

Wealth and equity have become enigmas. In most cases, people are just happy to get back to some semblance of what used to be normal. Expectations may be lower, but it's the mindset they've adopted to survive the career shift. Dwelling on the reality of the situation is too painful and too embarrassing. Most people aren't even conscious of the fact that they've given up on their dreams. Settling has become the "new normal."

In our four earlier cases, John, the baby boomer, decides that he and his wife can't travel like they dreamed of doing when they retired; and they must "live within their means" after John has retired and his pension will barely cover their bills. Despite her rigid work schedule, Beth has resigned herself to staying in her current job because she believes that finding a new one in her industry will be impossible. Similarly, Doug puts off proposing to his girlfriend out of concern for his lingering college debts. And Emily realizes that, if she wants her children to have a good college education, she'll have to sacrifice spending time with them in order to work the longer hours needed to get the high-paying promotion. Each of these people feel they have to compromise or give up their dreams and settle for whatever meager handouts the corporate world is willing to offer them.

These outcomes don't have to be a foregone conclusion. John, Beth, Doug and Emily can write a different story. They can opt to take control of your lives; and so can you. By educating yourself, learning about your options, and defining your goals and dreams, you can empower yourself to build the level of Income, Lifestyle, Wealth, and Equity you desire.

Polishing Your Dreams

Think of your dreams like a silver tea set given to you by your grandparents. Wanting to protect this treasure and afraid it may get broken, you hide it away in the china cabinet and then forget you even have it. As time passes, you assume it's lost until one day you happen to find it. It may be heavily tarnished, but once you polish it, you realize you still have a wonderful treasure. Your dreams are your treasures; they will guide you to the actions required to achieve them, but first you need to clarify them.

The Big Questions

To clarify your dreams, you need to look deep inside. You need to take that tea set out and inspect it closely. Let's begin by asking some big questions to help you paint an exact picture of the future you want.

First, how would you describe your feelings about your present career? More often than not, the answer to this question is simply frustration. Long hours, less pay, and no security for the future combine to create a sense of dissatisfaction that eventually becomes too irritating to ignore—that grain of sand we mentioned earlier. Take time and think about this question. Don't just use one word to answer it; instead, describe how it makes you feel. We tend to run away from things that are uncomfortable or that produce pain. Now is not the time to do that. You want to become completely aware of exactly the way your current situation makes you feel.

Next, explore the following questions: *What do you want more of in your life, personally and professionally? And conversely: What do you want less of?* Most people want more income and more free time, although your answers could be anything; it's your dream you're clarifying. For example, at a personal level, you may want to travel more, have more time to learn another language, be present at your children's functions and sport events, or be able to volunteer. In your career, you may seek more personal fulfillment, or perhaps less time dealing with your boss' whims or your subordinates' drama. These two questions help you hone in on exactly the kind of lifestyle you want, and eventually they bring clarity to the career path that will work best for you.

With these first questions answered, more detailed introspection can begin. *Five years from now, if you stay on your current career path, how do you see your options? How do you see yourself achieving financial independence? What are your biggest concerns about changing careers? If you knew you couldn't fail, what career would you choose?*

These kinds of questions immediately generate strong emotions, and emotions can be powerful motivators, empowering you to make a change. These questions elicit a chemical reaction—an almost visceral response—that helps you create your own detailed picture of the life and career you really want –a clear picture of your dreams.

YOU 2.0®

Consider the following question: *If we looked at your life a year from today, what has to have happened during that period, both personally and professionally, for you to be happy with your progress?* Creating the new version of yourself—your YOU 2.0®—requires you to identify the following three aspects of your life: Your Dangers, Opportunities and Strengths. Once you know what they are, the next step is to create a goal that will assist you in dealing with or taking advantage of these circumstances so you can achieve the Income, Lifestyle, Wealth and Equity you desire.

Dangers

Dangers are those things that keep you up at night. They are the obstacles and issues that you may be facing right now or in the future that worry you and make you feel you have no options and no control. They include:

- How much longer will I be employable?

- How much more limited will my career options get as time goes by?
- Is my age a limitation? Am I considered too old by employers? Will I ever get another job at my age?
- Can I really afford to wait to take control of my destiny?
- Are my current skills transferable?
- Do I have any opportunity to build the wealth and equity I desire for me and my family?
- How will I be able to fund my longer and active life expectancy? Will I end up depending on my children?
- Will the value of my investments and savings keep going down until I have nothing left for my retirement?
- How long will I be able to keep my current job? Will there be any other positions available if I lose my job?

What other probable or current circumstance creates sleepless nights for you?

Now, it's time to get proactive. You are not a victim of your circumstances. You have the power to take control of your life and change your destiny. For each of the dangers you identified above as applicable to you, create a goal that will empower and allow you to change these obstacles into your dream protection shields.

Opportunities

Opportunities are those circumstances or possibilities in your life that motivate you. These are the things that get you excited. Your life is filled with opportunities and possibilities. Sometimes the obstacles in our lives prevent us from seeing the many opportunities that surround us. Some of the opportunities you may want to focus on include:

- Your ability to take control of your destiny
- Your desire to spend more time on the things that matter most to you
- Your dream to reach your desired Income, Lifestyle, Wealth, and Equity.
- Your commitment to one day be financially independent
- Your aspiration to mitigate your risks and fast-track your career
- Your attention on creating the lifestyle of your dreams
- Your determination to fund your longer and active life expectancy
- Your curiosity to discover new possibilities beyond your current experiences
- Your yearning to be re-energized and passionate about life and your career

- Your longing to have the time and financial ability to give back to your community

What are other opportunities that excite you and make you want to change your circumstances?

It's time to leave behind the dread of paralyzing fear and relish on the hope that the new you–your YOU 2.0® can bring into your life. It's time to focus on what you want and not on what keeps you in the past. For each of the opportunities that resonated with you, identify the actions you will have to take in order to transform them from longings to reality.

Strengths

Strengths are your unique talents, capabilities, and skills that you need to identify and acknowledge so you can utilize them as you create the new version of yourself–YOU 2.0®. Your strengths become the tools you'll use to uncover the person that you need to be to achieve your dreams–your desired Income, Lifestyle, Wealth, and Equity. Too often we focus only on what we must change, on our weakness, and fail to recognize our assets. Right now it's time to identify the latter which include the following:

- All the success you have had in your current and previous jobs

- Your good health, energy, and vitality
- Your large circle of influence and strong community of peers
- Your ability to make sound decisions
- Your impeccable work ethics
- Your numerous transferable skills
- Your long record of accomplishments
- Your high degree of integrity
- Your possibilities mindset
- Your positive attitude
- Your strong belief that you can succeed at everything on which you focus your attention
- Your resilience: your ability to adapt and to embrace change

What other strengths do you have that will help you become YOU 2.0® so you can achieve your dreams?

Once you've taken stock of your strengths, your next step is to strategize how you can use them to create the new you--YOU 2.0®. For each one of your identified assets, describe how you plan to utilize them in your strategy. How will they help you write your success story?

Now that you've asked all these questions and have created your goals, once again create a picture in your mind of yourself a year from now, living the life you've always wanted. Think of the steps that got you there. A key component of this experience is to get beyond your current circumstances, to set your mind free, to give yourself permission to dream and to envision the future you want. Our YOU 2.0® worksheet summarizes the process we have discussed here. No matter how dire or isolating your circumstances appear to be, remember that you are not alone. Hundreds of thousands, and maybe even millions, of people today are dealing with similar, if not the same, issues. The YOU 2.0® worksheet is the result of working with people just like you for over 30 years.

YOU 2.0™

Powered by
THE ENTREPRENEUR'S SOURCE®
"Your success is our only business"™

If we looked at your life a year from today, what has to have happened during that period, both personally and professionally, for you to be happy with your progress?

NAME _____

DATE _____

EMAIL _____

Dangers

We have found that these are the common obstacles and issues people like you are facing.

Check all that are relevant to you, and add others if needed

- How long will I be employable?
- Conventional career options are more limited.
- Age factor limitations.
- Can I afford to wait to take control of my destiny?
- Are my current skills transferable?
- Little to no opportunity to build wealth and equity.
- How will I fund my longer and active life expectancy?
- Value of savings, investments, retirement has declined.
- Jobs today are very short lived.
- Declining career economy.
- ◯
- ◯

From the above choices, note your
TOP 3 DANGERS and fill in GOALS

DANGERS	GOALS

Opportunities

As well as obstacles, you have many opportunities you would like to be freed up to focus on.

Check all that are relevant to you, and add others if needed

- To control my own destiny.
- To spend more time on things that matter most.
- To reach my desired income, lifestyle, wealth, and equity.
- To reach my goal of financial freedom.
- To mitigate my risks and fast-track my new career.
- To focus and create the lifestyle of my dreams.
- To fund my longer and active lifestyle.
- To discover new possibilities beyond my current experiences.
- To be re-energized & be passionate.
- To give back within my community.
- ◯
- ◯

From the above choices, note your
TOP 3 OPPORTUNITIES and fill in GOALS

OPPORTUNITIES	GOALS

Strengths

You may have talents, capabilities, and skills that you would like to reinforce and maximize.

Check all that are relevant to you, and add others if needed

- I have been successful in my career to date.
- I have strong community, peers, and circle of influence.
- I make good choices, then go to work & make good decisions.
- My work ethic will not let me fail.
- I have strong transferable skills.
- I am healthy and vital.
- I have a strong record of accomplishments.
- I have a high degree of integrity.
- I am possibilities focused, I succeed in everything I put my mind to.
- I am adaptable and embrace change.
- ◯
- ◯

From the above choices, note your
TOP 3 STRENGTHS and fill in GOALS

STRENGTHS	GOALS

CHAPTER 3: WHAT HOLDS YOU BACK
(Common Obstacles in the Way of Your Financial Freedom)

If the road towards self-sufficiency and financial free-dom was free of obstacles and challenges most everyone would take it. However, in 2009 only 1 out of 9 workers was self-employed.4 Just making the choice to explore options can be confusing and scary. The sheer magnitude of choices can seem overwhelming. To add to this confusing array, there are many emotions that rear their ugly heads during this process.

As a result, when you begin considering options outside the traditional job market, you may have to contend with some or all of what we at The Entrepreneur's Source call "The F-words." On the road to your financial independence most of these F-words can hold you back if you are not careful; they are the obstacles you'll most likely have to face. The F-words include: Frustration, Fear, Financial Constraints, and sometimes even Family and Friends. The important thing to remember is that you can overcome all of these roadblocks if you focus on the most important F-word of all: Financial Freedom.

Frustration

Are you feeling under-appreciated? How about feeling left out of important decisions or stymied by bureaucratic flab? Are you in a dead-end job, waiting your turn for that pink slip? Do you ever feel you could do great things if you could run the show? These circumstances all lead to frustration.

When it comes to frustration, there are two kinds: healthy and unhealthy. The healthy type of frustration can be a motivator, while the unhealthy kind can be paralyzing. For people suffering from the latter type, frustration becomes a dark cloud that follows them around and prevents them from taking control of their lives. At some level, people suffering from unhealthy frustration start to like the state of frustration, because they begin to believe that it affords them the right to point the finger somewhere else.

You probably have met people who are suffering from this kind of frustration. They are the ones that cut you off on the highway and exhibit road rage. They are the ones that huff and puff when the checkout lines at the grocery store are too long and the cashiers are not fast enough for them. They are the ones who let their level of professional frustration spill over into their entire lives. But the truth is that most of these people may have been, and may actually still be, courteous and positive, but their career situations have gotten so out of hand that they feel they can't help themselves, and being rude seems their only release valve.

By now you know that these people can choose differently; they can start to explore other options that will help them feel more in control of their lives. However, for many of them, fear may not allow them to consider the fact that there are always other options that can decrease, and in most cases, eliminate the causes of their current frustration levels.

Which type of frustration are you feeling? Whether your frustration is the healthy or unhealthy kind, you can learn to turn your frustration into fascination so you can start to explore the options you have to reach the desired F-Word: Financial Freedom.

Fear

What do you worry about? What makes you afraid? What causes anxiety for you? What keeps you away from making a change? What makes you run the other way when someone brings the word "change" up? Are you even aware of all the voices of fear, and all of its disguises? Let's find out.

For over three decades, we have worked with people going through career transitions. We have assisted them fulfill their dreams and become self-sufficient. And, as we've accompanied them on the way to their goals, we have met all of their fears. Most people, at their career transition junction, worry about everything: from whether or not they will be employable once they reach a certain age, to doubts about the transferability of their skills in a time when traditional career options are becoming increasingly limited. Others worry about the change they are about to go through while being terrified of the big unknown that self-employment is for them. Most of these fears are fueled by false evidence that seems to be true. The acronym we often use for this mental state is F.E.A.R. (False Evidence Appearing Real.)

Once we get outside our comfort zone, our anxiety levels and insecurities start to rise. This is normal. This happens to most everyone. As a result, we start looking for reasons why something will not work, and manufacture scenarios that we call "evidence" to talk ourselves out of taking the necessary steps toward change. We create our own F.E.A.R.—our own False Evidence and make it Appear Real.

But, let's just remember that any time we learn how to do something new or different, it will, at first, be uncomfortable. The important questions at this point are: *"Is it worth it to you to be temporarily uncomfortable if the potential results will exceed your current results? Are you looking to be one hundred percent comfortable or are you looking to be successful in achieving your desired Income, Lifestyle, Wealth, and Equity?"*

We'll use the example of one of our clients, Stephen, to examine some of the common fears that prevent most people from exploring their options and choosing a different path to attain their goals and dreams. Bear in mind that a little fear is normal when you contemplate something new. But fears should not paralyze you. Remember, the answer to fear is information and support, which we give you throughout the coaching experience and the Journey of Discovery.

Fear of Change

For many people, change is a source of fear—the fear of added stress, the fear of discomfort, and the fear of the unknown. Yet, change is an inevitable part of life. Those who view it with fear tend to spend far too much energy trying *unsuccessfully* to avoid it. In fact in today's digital economy, change is the driving force.

Change seems frightening because it threatens the comfort we have constructed for ourselves. Feeling at risk, we try to create situations that we think will make us whole again, conditions and thoughts that will bring us back to the sense of security we used to feel. You can try to avoid that which seems to be bringing on the change, but today that avoidance is simply impossible. Sooner or later change will catch up with you. So the only way is to feel the fear and go through it anyway. Doing so becomes easier if we have a person we trust to support us.

The only way to overcome the fear of change is to have your eye on the ultimate goal, on your dream of financial independence for you and for your family. And, we will help you do just that.

Fear of the Big Unknown: Self-Employment

The fear of the unknown can also leave people in a frozen state—afraid of entering and exploring the new ground because they think they might get in trouble. They are afraid of losing what they are familiar with by jumping into the unknown, even when the familiar has reached a point of being unbearable. These people may know what they need to do, but they simply can't take action because they think the risk involved with their career transition is too big.

The irony is that, in today's job market, self-employment is probably the less risky choice. In fact, once you start to learn about your options, you will learn what works and what doesn't work for you, and you will soon gain clarity about what you need to do to achieve your desired Income, Lifestyle, Wealth, and Equity.

The idea of self-employment can be a terrifying thing for many reasons. While looking at new opportunities, people can feel pressured to make a decision, either to stay in their old jobs with the hope that the steady paychecks will continue, or to take a risk and strike out on their own. As human beings, we often fear making decisions because most of us equate "decision making" with "making a bad decision." In essence, the fear of self-employment is very much about the fear of making the wrong choice.

The fact that tales of business failures abound is not helpful to the decision-making process. Everyone has heard horror stories about the number of people who start their own businesses, only to have them go under after three, five, or even ten years. As a result, many people associate being self-employed with a much higher risk of failure. Individuals fear being self-employed because they cannot escape the sense of insecurity that arises from the lack of a perceived corporate safety net. They wonder if they can truly do this on their own where others have failed.

Another misconception that relates to fear of self-employment is the belief that, in order to succeed, you must love what you do or have a background, a passion, or the experience in that type of business. This unfounded belief misguides many individuals to spend countless hours searching for "the right" business that best fits their passion, interests, prior experience, and skills.

What many people don't realize is that everything they enjoy doing now didn't particularly interest them until after they had experienced it. For example, you may never have considered learning to golf until someone talked you into taking lessons. You may have dismissed it and called it a "silly game" until you actually tried it. Once you got over your preconceptions and gave it a try, you might have discovered that you really love the game of golf.

As human beings, we don't like to leave our comfort zones, but if we simply take a chance and keep an open mind to something new, we may find a more fulfilling career than anything the corporate world has to offer. The only way to beat the fear of the unknown is to take the first step. If you're afraid of getting in trouble, remember that you're already in bigger trouble. If you listen to the voice of your fears, you'll live an empty life. But, if you listen to the voice of your heart, you'll live a remarkable life.

Fear of Success

Believe it or not, fear of success stops more people than the fear of failure. Sure, we tend to be more aware of our fear of failing—the pain involved with that is usually more tangible, the images more vivid. In many ways, this is part of the unconscious mind's brilliant strategy to keep us from seeing the real fear–the fear that we can be a total success.

Success has all kinds of repercussions and these by-products are the real causes of our fears. It is not success per se that we are afraid of; we're terrified of what we believe it will mean. With success come higher expectations, possible jealousy from others and, the most dreaded consequence of all, change. Who will we become when we get to be successful? How will our lives change? What about our families? How will our relationships be affected by our success? When we consider these questions, sometimes failing seems like a cakewalk in comparison.

It's important that you identify what you're truly afraid of so you can collect the evidence to dismantle your fears. Learning about your options with a sense of curiosity and not dread will empower you, and with each new piece of information, you'll start dissolving your fears.

Finances

The next F-word is Finances. There are many ways to finance a business, safely and confidently. Even in the last five years when banks basically stopped lending, there were still ways to finance a business investment. Opportunities are there for all types of people and their varied financial situations. Don't make up your mind before you explore your options. For more than 30 years, we have witnessed people, who thought they would never get money to open a business, somehow find the money they needed to make their dream come true. Get the facts; don't dismiss your dream for the fear that you could never afford having your own business.

Family and Friends

The last of the F-words is family and friends, who are perhaps the most important influences on whether or not we decide to take the leap of faith and leave behind the traditional career. This is especially true of those families dependent on that person as the main breadwinner.

It's of course an important factor to consider the opinion and feelings of those we love when deciding on our future career paths. After all, they will also be affected by our choices. However, family and friends can become a significant roadblock to seizing your destiny and taking control of your Income, Lifestyle, Wealth and Equity.

All your life, your family has relied on you, and possibly only you, to provide the security and stability they need to live and be happy. When something happens to undermine that ability to provide, such as the emergence of a changing job market and the disappearance of your traditional career options, a sense of shame and doubt can emerge with the knowledge that your family knows you may no longer have the ability to provide for them at the same level you always have done before. It's the elephant in the room that no one really talks about, and it could potentially exacerbate your fears about attempting to transfer into a more proactive and self-sufficient career.

Your family and friends aren't deliberately trying to pull you down. They just don't want you to fail. There is a pretty good chance they are stuck in the old paradigm, and even though you are now bold enough to say, *"The old way isn't working anymore, and I need to find a new way,"* they may try to discourage you because they are suffering from the same fears and obstacles as you were.

Think of it like crabs in a basket. If you have ever been crabbing, you know that after you put a layer or two of crabs in a basket, you no longer need a lid because whenever one of the crabs goes to climb out, the rest of the crabs reach up and pull it back down. Although it may look like they are trying to keep the potential escapee in the basket, what is really happening is that they are hanging on in hopes that they'll be able to get out with their compatriot.

The crabs have the desire to escape but are too caught up in the old methods to see that what they are doing is harming more than helping. In much the same way, your family and friends may be holding you back because they are fearful of being left behind.

We all want to be part of something—a family, a group of friends, coworkers—and they may make it even harder for you especially when you already have doubts and reservations. In addition to your own fears, others want to protect you from what seems to be certain catastrophe to them by expressing pessimistic opinions that create a negative multiplier effect, which in turn generates more F.E.A.R. (False Evidence that Appears Real). A vicious cycle that turns into a stagnant career path is thus created and maintained by the influence of our family and friends.

Therefore, it's of utmost importance that you involve your family early in your Journey of Discovery. In many ways, it will become their own journey.

It Is All in the Timing

No matter what fears people may or may not have about venturing into the sometimes daunting world of self-sufficiency, some of them will always find a way of putting off taking that final leap. More often than not, once they've addressed all of the potential fears, choosing a path becomes an issue of timing.

In three decades of empowering people, regardless of how good or bad the economy and job market have been, we have found that some people have always used one or the other as an excuse to say, "This isn't the right time to leave the conventional career path." If things have been going well with the market and new businesses are flourishing, they don't want to risk the increased competition. If the economy has been on a downslide, they do not think starting a business is financially viable. After all, why risk starting something that will likely be wiped out by a recession?

No matter what, there is always a reason. They want a 100 percent guarantee in a world where nothing is 100 percent guaranteed. They want to disprove every opportunity in order to keep from facing the hardest fact of all—that the only things keeping them from the success of that opportunity are their own fears—fears that are most often unfounded. Sometimes we need to be okay with the fact that all we can do is make the best possible choice and then all we have left is to get started and make it a good decision.

Moving Into the Future

Most people see the gap between their current situation and income and the success that they envision in the future, and say, *"I don't know if I can survive that leap."* They are busy focusing on the gap instead of on the other side and thus their fears take over and win. A coach can help create a safety net so you can make the jump.

An ever-increasing number of people are taking the

leap from *unEmployment to Empowerment*®. We see our main role to be helping you envision what it is like when you take control and use your own business as a vehicle to attain the life you desire. Your job is to embark on the Journey of Discovery to learn about your options and what is possible.

CHAPTER 4: **MAKING YOUR YOU 2.0® REAL**
(Choosing the Right Vehicle to Your Dream)

Thus far we have guided you through a Journey of Discovery first by taking a close look at the circumstances that brought you to this point of inquiry and pursuit of something better. We then continued by taking you inward and asking some critical questions to help you create and clarify the new version of yourself–your YOU 2.0®. We then went deeper and examined the most common obstacles people face when questioning their life choices. We showed you that you are not alone, that the things that may be keeping you back, such as conscious and unconscious fears and the influence of those you love, are common barriers faced by most everyone considering change, regardless of what type of change it is. Now it's time to start looking outside again but with a different perspective–one of being empowered to change your circumstance by the choices you make.

Unless we have been born rich, most of us have to engage in some kind of activity that generates the income we need to live. We need to have a vehicle that will get us the Income, Lifestyle, Wealth and Equity we desire. The options available to us include: the job market, the stock market and real estate investments, and owning a business. The latter choice, owning a business, has two flavors. Either you go at it alone or you choose to invest in a franchise opportunity and get the benefits of a proven system and the support and training you need to be successful.

The Job Market

We have spent a great deal of time exploring the hopeless state of the job market and what the Career Revolution has meant for most employees and probably for you as well. You already know that there is no longer job security–that jobs are lost every day to economic fluctuations, cheaper labor, new technology, younger workers and so on. Many people feel cheated by the trade-offs they have to make working in the corporate world. However, even though the job market is not what it used to be, there are still some good jobs out there. There are a few companies that care for, challenge, and fairly compensate their employees, even when they aren't the norm any longer.

Let's face it; some people are made to be employees. They like the structure of that type of relationship. They are comfortable with not having any control and they actually prefer it this way. They don't mind having a boss even when most of the time they think they make better decisions than their supervisors. They can and enjoy focusing on the task of their 9 to 5 jobs that may go much longer than eight hours, but they feel they can go home and leave their jobs behind. There is nothing wrong with them; that's just who they are. We need people who are willing and happy to be employees. We need people who prefer routine, whose choice is to shun responsibility of the greater picture and to focus only on what they have to do that day, that moment. Our economic structure depends on having a variety of preferences and choices. So, despite whatever uncertainties the job market has to offer, it may still be the best choice for you even when survival may have added an undesirable layer of stress.

The Stock Market and Real Estate Investments

Being an investor is another option available when exploring career paths, even when it may not be for everyone. It takes the right type of personality to be a successful investor. The stock and the real estate markets fluctuate with the economy and require not only interest, knowledge, and aptitude in these fields, but also a high tolerance for the risk and the lack of control inherent in these reactive investment vehicles. For most of us, investing is a way to diversify our income and wealth creating efforts. We simply don't see it as a full time occupation—the risk is just too great to rely solely on this activity. However, for some people, this reactive vehicle of creating the desired Income, Lifestyle, Wealth and Equity is the right one.

Owning a Business

The final option is self-employment–owning a business as the vehicle to create your desired Income, Lifestyle, Wealth, and Equity—to go from *unEmployment to Empowerment*®. You can take the journey of business ownership alone or you can choose to have a support team by your side, as is the case when you invest in a franchise.

Independent business ownership requires knowledge, systems, resources, and expertise. Before you even open your doors for business, you can incur significant costs and need to gain required knowledge associated with market research, equipment, store design and layout, pricing, public relations, testing the model, putting an infrastructure in place, developing technology, hiring and training employees. An independent business owner has to know or learn about many different aspects of starting and operating a business that have nothing to do with the services or products it offers. Independent business owners have to know about marketing, finance, accounting, operations, customer service, equipment, vendor relations, price negotiations, pricing, employee management, and customer retention, among many other disciplines. They also have to keep ahead of the competition, and spend money and resources in research and development to stay ahead of the game. They have to create demand for their products and services by building a strong brand. If they want to succeed and they don't have all of this knowledge and experience, they have to get it somewhere else—they will have to hire employees or experts in these areas which can be very expensive.

Independent business owners have to develop and prove their business model; they don't have a successful example to follow. They may be able to get some information about similar businesses, but they don't have the internal scoop— the "secret sauce". If they don't do well, they have no way of knowing what may be causing the problem, so most small independent business owners just blame the economy or the competition from the large franchise chains. But what if their failure to achieve the results they want and need has something to do with what they are or aren't doing? Unless they hire an outside management consultant or business coach, they have no way of knowing what may be the cause of the problem.

One of the most disturbing characteristics of owning an independent business is the fact that you are all alone. There is no support mechanism behind you, no one to call when you have a question or a problem, no one who can listen to your woes and help you get out of your own way to achieve the results you desire. There is no one to provide training when there is a gap, no one to even recognize when there is a gap–it's just you. This is especially distressing if you are accustomed to working for someone else or in a team environment.

There are some lone rangers out there for whom not having a support team is not a problem. These people prefer to be alone and to have full responsibility for everything. They are risk takers and love to wear many hats. They thrive on the pursuit of opportunity. They are the true entrepreneurs and you, perhaps, fit that mold.

However, for the great majority of people, being totally independent and creating a business from scratch has little appeal. Having a successful, proven roadmap to follow and a team to support us in our own business is important for most of us. The good news is that you don't have to be all alone and solely responsible for every facet of the business to own and operate one. *Franchising allows you to be in business for yourself but not by yourself.*

The great majority of franchise companies started as a business that reached a certain level of success and then decided to scale it up by sharing their secret winning formula with people who are willing to follow their proven system. Franchisors (the companies that franchised their businesses) share their experience with franchisees (those people who invest in the opportunity) by providing them with comprehensive training and support programs and the roadmap needed to replicate business results.

Most franchising opportunities require no experience or background in their business and industry. In fact most franchise companies prefer people who have no prior experience in their type of business to join as franchisees. Why is that? It is rather simple; franchising is all about replicating a business' success through a proven SYSTEM–a model that affords you to Save Yourself Significant Time, Energy and Money.

Franchising is one of the few commercial interactions based on creating and sustaining a win-win relationship. The success of a franchise company depends on the success of its franchisees and vice versa. This interdependence tends to create a healthy family environment where members support instead of compete with each other, and where they motivate, celebrate, and are ready to assist other franchisees.

Although the premises of franchising apply to all franchise companies, franchise opportunities and companies are not created equal, nor are they right for everyone. The potential for win-win relationships, for support and for a successful formula and winnings tools is there in every company, but each concept is different and how these elements manifest in the company depends on many factors. So, if you have concluded that franchising might be the right vehicle for you to achieve the Income, Lifestyle, Wealth and Equity you desire, you still have a lot of work ahead of you. You need to discern which opportunity suits you best.

This is the point where things may feel overwhelming. After all, there are thousands of franchise opportunities to choose from. You may be thinking: *Where do I start? How many opportunities do I need to investigate? When do I know that I have found the right opportunity? How do I know I am making the right decision?*

These are all logical questions when we are in problem-solving mode. But this is not where you are right now. You need to change your way of thinking and see this journey as a learning process not a decision-making one. And, you need to consider that you don't have to go through this journey alone. The Entrepreneur's Source has helped tens of thousands of people just like you make successful career transitions and find the franchise opportunity that has helped them achieve their desired Income, Lifestyle, Wealth, and Equity. We welcome the opportunity to assist you in accomplishing the same. And, as you continue on your journey, the answers to these questions will become clear.

CHAPTER 5: THE COACHING EXPERIENCE — NO NEED TO GO ALONE

Oprah Winfrey has a coach. Phil Mickelson has a coach. Bill Gates has a coach. So, why shouldn't you have one?

Whether it's a personal coach, a sports coach, a business coach, or a career transition coach, successful people enlist the assistance of these professional specialized resources. The more successful you are, the more you realize that you can't be an expert at everything. We are all students and we're constantly learning and growing—a coach provides the safe environment, the challenge, and the accountability to allow you to reach your maximum potential. Perhaps this is the reason that 47 percent of organizations see coaching as essential to their executive decision-making process according to a Right Management Consultants survey, and their research shows that this number grows every year.

A coach does three important things:

- A coach creates awareness of what is and what could be possible for you
- A coach provides the education and environment you need to examine areas of your life that hold the answer to your future; and,
- A coach holds you accountable for your goals, needs, and expectations

The coaches of The Entrepreneur's Source specialize in alternative career options and career transition, and we have been doing so for over 30 years. Our coaching experience helps you see beyond your blind spots and challenges you to explore what lies outside your comfort zone. Let's face it, generally, we only allow ourselves to see things we understand or about which we have firsthand knowledge. Our coaching experience is designed to help people like you to look inside and determine whether or not they are currently achieving their career and lifestyle goals; and, if they are not, to find options that works best for them. For most people, these options are nothing they had considered previously.

Some of your options may be intimidating at first because you have no experience in them and thus lack a frame of reference. You may have bought into someone's story and believe it, so you can justify your fears. You are at a point in your life, however, that calls for having an open mind, so you can gather the information you need to find what you are seeking—to discover a better way. For example, business ownership may produce all kinds of fear. And, in the face of fear, it is natural that your mind starts to search for those examples of businesses that went under or stories about business failure you have read in the paper or heard about from a friend. But just because something is scary, it does not mean you shouldn't explore it and educate yourself. Knowledge is the only weapon against fear. Fear simply dissolves in the face of information, facts, and knowledge. The power of working with a coach is that you learn to see things differently than you have ever seen them before. And at the end of the day, wouldn't you rather make informed choices based on facts rather than emotions?

Leadership, Relationship, and Opportunity

In the last couple of decades we have lost trust in the organizations and institutions we have considered and chosen to be our leaders; namely, our government, Wall Street, the media, and corporations. The world where a handshake and your word meant everything has disappeared and been replaced by one where due diligence and mistrust are the guiding principles. We crave for leaders we can trust and for relationships with people we can rely on to have our best interest in mind at all times. These trustworthy sources can show us opportunities we would have missed otherwise. Leadership, relationship, and opportunity are the three pillars of our coaching experience.

Leadership

At the beginning of the Journey of Discovery when we investigate where we have been and the conditions the Career Revolution brought about, most people are looking at leadership from the standpoint of, *"Who can lead me out of this mess?"* They are afraid of the complexity of the journey and, most likely, have started on this path many times before just to turn back as their fear dragons started to show up. They know that if they try to go at this alone again, they will probably never reach those distant goals on their horizon. They are looking for the kind of leadership that provides direction and a safe space to recognize that this is all new and that they don't have to know everything—a space where learning can take place.

The coaching experience of The Entrepreneur's Source is designed to lead you through these peaks and valleys of doubt and fear. We help you by providing the structure by which you can find your internal compass that will lead you on your journey. And, if for any reason you start to dismiss your internal directional guidance, we bring you back to what's important to you.

Relationship

While leadership begins by asking, "Who can give me direction?" the relationship factor asks the equally important question, "Who can I trust?" Some people feel like they have fallen through the trap door of corporate America and now have come to the quick realization that the systems, institutions, and organizations on which they had depended in the past are no longer reliable. So, who can they trust with their vision of the future?

Our coaching methodology helps to fill this void, introducing you to a win-win relationship. This relationship shapes as a byproduct of empowering our clients to see their options clearly and working to create a bond that eventually brings them back to a place of trust. This relationship opens up a world of possibilities.

Opportunity

Once leadership and relationship have been established, our clients can begin to see beyond their blind spots and embrace possibilities they never considered before or that they had previously dismissed. They are more open to education and exploration, which brings opportunity, the final key foundational factor, into play.

Working with a trusted coach who provides direction makes it easy for our clients to explore options in the safe space they have created together. They realize there is no pressure to make decisions about their career; they are merely embarking on a Journey of Discovery. Being able to see past their fears and frustrations allows them to focus clearly on new opportunities—on what lies ahead. In this environment, true change can take place and mindsets are transformed.

Tens of thousands of people have been empowered by The Entrepreneur's Source, our coaches, our system, and our coaching experience. The benefits of being aware of your options and non-conventional career choices are tremendous, even if you do not act on that knowledge immediately. Remarkably, 95 percent of our clients end up discovering options they admittedly would have never looked at on their own or would have prematurely dismissed.

From Seeking to Understanding

Let's look at the kind of coaching we provide and how we can help you see possibilities, which you may not have even known existed until now. We start the journey by inviting you to stop seeking outside of yourself for a while and to take time to think about where you are in your life and where you want to be. Together, we start to create the space where you can feel free to explore your life today and tomorrow without any fear or risk.

Although key elements such as leadership, relationships, and opportunities may have been missing from your life up to now, we provide the structure in which you can rediscover them. Within this structure, you can begin to clarify your objectives—dream your dreams—while knowing there are people supporting and guiding you along the way. Where are you in your career? How can you change your current situation? What motivates you? What would you do if you knew you could not fail? How would your family feel if you made the decision to try a new career path? Your journey with us is about helping you clarify all these things and more. Many times, your coach will ask you questions and draw you into conversations you haven't even had with your closest friends or spouse—frank discussions of how you see your future. It's about connecting on a human level and being able to question, listen, and explore.

We understand that you may still be nervous. It's perfectly normal. Stepping out of the traditional career mold and embarking on a new path can be a frightening prospect, and a coaching session certainly is not going to completely eliminate those fears. It would not be normal if you didn't feel some anxiety about leaving your comfort zone. However, the information we provide will certainly help you dissolve or mitigate the fears you feel during the journey.

What you need to keep in mind is that the fear and discomfort are only temporary. Would it be worth it to go through it all if you knew that the outcome of those first steps down the road toward self-sufficiency will be so much greater than simply remaining on your current path? Would it be worth it to get the information and education to help you clarify your options? Remember, knowledge dissolves fear.

One of the benefits of our coaching experience is that it allows people to reframe a situation that, at that moment, seems like the most terrible thing that has ever happened to them. The prospect of losing your job or the actual experience of losing it can be devastating. But what would happen if someone could help you see that it may not be as bad as you think—that what seems a totally hopeless situation is truly the beginning of hope. What if the saying: "You have to lose something to gain something" applies to your job and career? You might start considering that this dire situation you're in may be the start of a new rich and fulfilling life–an empowered one.

Critical Ingredients for a Successful Journey of Discovery

Once you have clarified where you have been, where you are, and where you want to go, we show you different business models. We don't expect you to fall in love with them. As a matter of fact, we don't expect you to even like them, at least at first. Many people when presented with business models feel they have to choose one. But this journey isn't about making decisions; it's about learning. By exploring these business options, by learning about what they have to offer and talking to people who are using these particular business options as the vehicle to their dream, you further clarify what you desire in your life. But you must remain open and have a beginner's mind. Yes, it sounds a bit Zen for a reason. Zen Master Suzuki said: *"In the beginner's mind there are many possibilities."* And, that's what we all want, isn't it?

Therefore, there are two important requirements to which we ask you to commit if you want to have a successful Journey of Discovery. They are:

#1: Keeping an open mind.

#2: Making no decisions.

Only under these two conditions can you reach your goals and your YOU 2.0® and go from *unEmployment to Empowerment®*. You will work against yourself and your possible future by making decisions and eliminating options prematurely. Our objective as your coaches is that you become aware of opportunities and examine concepts you might never have considered before. Things that you may have previously dismissed without proper examination can hold the key to your future success in achieving the Income, Lifestyle, Wealth and Equity you desire. So the key isn't to look for evidence to prove your preconceptions right, but instead it's to explore, to learn, and to be fascinated by the discovery of new information and options you hadn't ever thought possible before. Are you committed enough to your dreams to keep an open mind? If you aren't, there is little value anyone can provide to you.

Although we act as your guides throughout this journey,

you are still in charge of how fast or how slow you want to go. We will support you and challenge you to look beyond your blind spots as you work on defining your dream and as you learn about the possible vehicles to attain it. We will provide you with education and tools that help you get outside your comfort zone, but you must meet us half way by keeping an open mind and by not making premature decisions.

There are times that your coach will challenge you and hold you accountable to what you say you want. Often, it's just easier to quit and pretend like problems and dissatisfactions don't exist or that they don't affect us. Sometimes we believe it's better to avoid the issue rather than confront it. But if we are truthful to ourselves, we really know that avoidance doesn't solve the problem or make it go away. Our coaches will often have "carefrontations" with clients. We know it's tough and we know it's hard, but we are here for you. We believe everybody has a dream worth pursuing.

Remember, this is a time for exploration. Many people are too afraid of change to take this initial step, but you have seized the opportunity to explore the world of self-sufficiency and financial independence. Now you have to keep on the path that can take you there. We believe in: your Possibilities, your Options, and your Dreams. Do you?

Our Unique Coaching Methodology

Throughout this book, we have talked a great deal about bridging the gap between your current situation and a brighter future full of greater Income, Lifestyle, Wealth, and Equity, and of moving from *unEmployment to Empowerment*®. You may already be working side by side with your Entrepreneur's Source coach, and you now have developed an appreciation for why they do what they do. Or you may now be at a point where you are ready to engage your coach, so that you too can benefit from the value our coaching relationship brings. Let's take a look at what makes the relationship between The Entrepreneur's Source coaches and their clients so unique.

Believing in the Dream

A central characteristic of our coaches is that they often believe in your dream more than you do. How is that even possible? Let's think back to the weight loss analogy we used earlier in the book. We said that everybody knows what it takes to lose weight. By and large it involves eating less and exercising more. But what prevents most people from accomplishing their weight loss goals is the lack of the right habits and the discipline or will power to endure and keep the commitment in times of temptation or stress. Giving up on the desired result in the short term is almost always easier than developing the habits that will ultimately give you what you say you want, and wanting to be self-sufficient is no different than that. In addition, occasionally the dream can be beyond the blinders you have placed on yourself that prevent you from seeing your possibilities and options. Being blind to those possibilities doesn't mean there is anything wrong with you; it simply means that no one has given you the information you need to find a new or better path. This is where our coaches come into the picture.

The coach's role is to guide you into the land of possibilities and help you establish the right relationships by providing the leadership that will allow you to look at things from a different perspective. Every coach wants you to see the opportunities that exist beyond your comfort zone.

One of the key factors in our coaching methodology is that it isn't about selling you features or benefits. In fact, it is not about selling you anything. Our coaches are there solely to guide you to a place of clarity that you would normally not be able to reach on your own. It is about creating an environment and establishing that sense of leadership and relationship that will allow this discovery to happen.

Besides helping you reflect inward and gain clarity about what you want more of and less of in life and helping you reconnect with your primary aim, our coaching experience offers some real practical examples of business models for you to explore and learn about. It is at the point of looking at business models that most people forget about the commitments of having an open mind and making no decisions. Preconceptions and fear take over and you can too easily fall into their trap and forget that this is all about learning and not about deciding.

When presented with business models, many of our clients' first reactions include statements like: *"I don't like any of these. They have nothing to do with my experience or personality. I just don't like them. I thought you had been listening to me."* In most cases this is the voice of fear talking. The business models are probably unfamiliar to them and they can't picture themselves in them. The business concepts are forcing these clients out of their comfort zones and it's scary. Sometimes it's purely old programming. They may think picking a new career path is like falling in love. They are not exactly sure what they are looking for, but they think they will know it when they see it. These clients just have blind spots. Our job as their coach is to challenge them on what could be limiting beliefs, to shine a light on their blind spots, and to ensure that False Evidence Appearing Real doesn't hold them back from their greatness.

If you are worried that the same may happen to you and that your fears will keep you away from your goals, don't fret; we will remind you. We will make you aware of your blind spots and we will bring you back to what's important to you. For us it's all about making your dreams come true. Your success is our only business.

CHAPTER 6: THE FINAL STEPS
Embracing Your Financial Independence

Having experienced some of what The Entrepreneur's Source Journey of Discovery is about; thinking and planning what that next version of you, YOU 2.0®, is going to be; having defined your Income, Lifestyle, Wealth and Equity® goals a little better; having challenged some of your own perceptions about business ownership and what it takes to be self-sufficient—your next questions might simply be, "How does this all work? How do I go from what I have learned to owning a franchise?" In this chapter, we'll take a closer look at two of the perceived obstacles that can rear up in these final stages: funding and fear of decisions.

Financing the Future

You now understand that the emotions and fears you might be feeling are common to most people in your position. By now, the big question is probably, "How do I make this happen from a financial standpoint?"

Obviously, financing something like this is a major concern for most people, but it's important to keep in mind that part of this experience is learning how to turn your investments from reactive to proactive. In short, you need to invest in yourself and in your future.

There's no such thing as hopeless. After more than 30 years of helping people find ways to achieve their dreams, we have found that a high percentage of our clients are able to fund their business vehicles. It is simply a matter of moving beyond the "Yeah, but" phase—"Yeah, but those other people had money," or "Yeah, but I don't have any equity in my home and I lost a ton of money on my 401(k)." We won't allow you to dismiss your opportunities or give up on your dream because you believe your circumstances are unique. Just like the other fears and barriers you may have encountered along this path, the money question is one that can be dealt with and overcome.

Preparing for the Transition

Okay, so now you know you want to explore the world of self-sufficiency and you have walked across the bridge to see what it looks like on the other side: a world of greater and better Income, Lifestyle, Wealth, and Equity. For many people, the next question can be one of the most difficult. How do you fund your transition from *unEmployment to Empowerment*® while still maintaining the financial necessities of running a household?

Perhaps your kids take piano lessons or need money for college tuition. Maybe it's an even more basic need for something like groceries. Either way, if you are like most households, you have a monthly budget that needs to be met; therefore, intentionally leaving behind a steady paycheck, even with the prospect of self-sufficiency emerging on the horizon, can be a financially frightening idea.

The key here is to budget properly. If you were beginning a new job, in all likelihood, you would begin with a salary that would increase the longer you remained in your position or the more competently you handled the job. The transition phase from employee to self-employed works in the same way; essentially, you will be cutting yourself a paycheck. And, you have to plan that at first it will be a smaller paycheck than in the future.

At the beginning of your planning phase, sit down and draw up a monthly budget, figuring out exactly how much you and your family will need in order to maintain your lifestyle with all of its necessities and activities. Then think about what is possible for you to cut out or live without for a short period of time and figure out what's the length of time that you can live without those things.

Obviously, you don't want to go backwards and give up the things you need or love. But sometimes a temporary sacrifice can lead you to your ultimate goals. By finding a balance in your finances and budgeting the correct amount of money, you can determine whether or not you have enough to see your family through the transition phase. Ultimately, you will be investing in yourself and in them.

Funding Made Easy

Like financing, funding can be a major issue for many people, not because it's difficult to find but because most people are not aware of all the options that exist.

Often, *funding*—one of the looming F-words—is the elephant in the room when considering the possibility of self-sufficiency. A key element of The Entrepreneur's Source model is our determination to shift the paradigm of fear associated with that term. In fact, one of our goals is to help our clients view funding as an empowering part of the coaching process. It is not something to fear but to embrace.

So how do you get beyond funding?

The answer is in your Career Capital—in essence, everything you have done up to this point in your life. The key is to leverage funding for your future Income, Lifestyle, Wealth and Equity from your 401(k) plan to investments, savings, and real estate—everything that gives you net worth. Your family and friends can also provide a source of funding, so make sure to think about who can help you.

In today's new normal, many people have shifted their mindsets into a "scarcity mentality." Too many people haven't been producing any income or haven't been producing at the levels they once did. As a result, they're fearful of using that Career Capital, because they aren't looking at the return on that investment, just at the risk of finding their financial resources depleted.

Although the instinctive reaction in many cases is to not "spend" that capital on a franchise, in truth, you are not spending your Career Capital on anything. When you use it to finance a franchise, you are actually moving it from one line of net worth to another—turning it from a reactive investment into a proactive one. Over the last few years, reactive investments have been a roller coaster at best, and most people are tired of the bumpy ride. Franchise ownership re-empowers people with the confidence they need to seize their destiny and embrace a future of better Income, Lifestyle, Wealth and Equity.

Remember John, the baby boomer about to retire that we met in an earlier chapter? He has spent his entire career building his pension and setting aside money in his savings account. Although he knows that his careful planning has not left him quite enough for the retirement years, he worries about "spending" his savings and 401(k) on a franchise. What if the business fails? How will he survive if this latest investment doesn't work out? As John goes through our coaching journey and starts gathering information and understanding what it takes to go from *unEmployment to Employment*®, he realizes that he isn't spending money but simply reallocating funds to invest in himself—going from reactive to proactive.

To escape that scarcity mentality, you need to look back at your career achievements, everything you have made up your mind to do and at which you have been successful. Imagine what would happen if you moved those financial and emotional investments from reactive to proactive—investing in yourself instead of in someone else's profit. When seen from that vantage point, it's more of a risk not to invest in your future than to do it.

Know Your Options

One of the most prevalent misconceptions about funding is that there is only one way to do it. We seem to hear how difficult it is for most people to find a loan; but like so much else during these times, the traditional paths are no longer the only way to accomplish things. Even though many claim banks and other financial institutions are more stringent than ever in lending money, franchises are still getting funded.

Just as with every other aspect of The Entrepreneur's Source Journey of Discovery, the key to finding funding is in educating yourself on the options available to you. And we have the resources to help you in that exploration. In many cases, you do not have to rely on a single source of funding and can look to multiple avenues to achieve your financing.

In addition to your Career Capital, perhaps one of the franchise business models you are interested in is willing to offer some financing or leasing options. Or maybe part of the funding package for a brick-and-mortar business includes leasehold improvements and equipment. No matter what, there are numerous sources for finding funding outside the traditional avenues. It is simply a matter of exploration.

Decisions, Decisions, Decisions

Having covered one of the *final* F-word fears—*financing*—it's time to look at the other obstacle that can often creep up even after you have reached a point of clarity about what the best road ahead may be: fear of decisions.

For most people, the fear of decisions prevents them from pursuing their dreams and even from seeing possibilities. Or perhaps it can help to look at it in a slightly different way: people actually would be okay with making decisions if they knew they could always make the right decision. What people fear is making the wrong decision and having to live with the consequences. Nobody wants to make the wrong decision. That is why we have designed our Journey of Discovery to assist people reach a point of clarity where they realize they have gathered enough information and find themselves beyond the decision-making point. You too will know when you have reached that point. From time to time, however, a few clients start suffering from what we call "paralysis by analysis." For these people, their fear of making a decision keeps them searching for more facts and information even when deep inside they know they don't need any more data. Really what it boils down to is looking for a 100 percent guarantee where there is none. If you fall into this trap, your coach will help you review the information you have already gathered against what you have defined as your goals. There will be times that we will have to accept the fact that nobody can always make the right decision, but what we can do is make a decision and then start working at making it the right one.

All You Need Is Time

Many clients, when they come to The Entrepreneur's Source, are under the assumption that the entire experience will take a tremendous amount of time, especially in narrowing down their options. Some even use that presumption as an excuse not to take the Journey of Discovery, claiming they do not have the time. It is kind of like saying, "I don't have the time or I am too busy to develop healthier eating habits." If you are waiting for the perfect time, it will like never arrive. Just do or learn one thing a day about what it will take to go from *unEmployment to Empowerment*®.

Since this is your Journey of Discovery, you set the pace. This experience accommodates even the busiest work, life, or travel schedule. You will typically meet telephonically for about an hour or so a week with your coach. Although reaching a point of clarity varies from person to person. You cannot force discovery, and like an insight, you never quite know when it is going to hit you. But if you stick with the journey, you will reach that point of clarity, when you know exactly what you must do. This is not a fear-free state, but it is a state of excitement when you know the action to take and you will go through the fear and make it happen.

Many times coaches say they can literally see the relief wash over clients after they have reached that point of clarity—they know what they have accomplished. We have not done it; they have.

This is the resounding success of The Entrepreneur's Source: leading clients from *unEmployment to Empowerment*. Are you ready to embark on your Journey? What will your YOU 2.0® look like? If you looked at your life a year from today, what has to have happened during that period, both personally and professionally, for you to be happy with your progress?

The successful completion of this journey towards your dreams is our only business.

CHAPTER 7: **CASE STUDIES**

By now, you have read about what you need to do to get to your desired Income, Lifestyle, Wealth and Equity and to your YOU 2.0®. You have a good idea of what is involved with The Entrepreneur's Source Journey of Discovery. Now might be a good time to look at some experiences of what it is like to go through this process from beginning to end with the help of some real-life examples. All names and some of the circumstances have been changed to protect the privacy of our clients.

Kevin

PR executive Kevin came to The Entrepreneur's Source after deciding that he was dissatisfied with his current high paying ad firm job. At 50 years of age, he had three kids heading for college and a wife whose job didn't earn enough to support the family on its own. At Kevin's first coaching session, one of our coaches asked him to give a brief sketch of his job—what he liked about it, what he hated, and what finally motivated him to seek out other options.

It was at that point that Kevin began his Journey of Discovery. Over the next several weeks, he would take a close look at his life and job and try to find the reasons he was contemplating a change. For Kevin, and many people like him, this can be a difficult experience involving some real soul searching. But Kevin had an Entrepreneur's Source Coach who introduced him to tools that helped Kevin crystallize what he desired in his life.

Kevin may not have been able to pinpoint the reasons for his dissatisfaction immediately; however, the more time he took to think about it, the more he came to realize that he was tired of the long business trips, the time he missed out on spending with his family, and the continual worry that no matter how good he was at his job or how many hours he put in with his company, it was very likely that he would eventually get a pink slip anyway like so many of his friends had in recent years. In short, he was tired of feeling like he had no control over his life and tired of being forced to work so hard for what, at the end of the day, was actually someone else's dream.

The more Kevin thought about it, the more he began to imagine what his future might hold—what he wanted his life to look like five years down the line. Did he want a career that challenged him more creatively or intellectually? Did he want to have the free time to go to his son's football game without worrying or hurrying back to the office for yet another interminable conference call? Could he picture himself running his own business, controlling his own destiny?

Once Kevin began exploring his dreams for the future,

he also started to consider how those closest to him would react to his new goals. Knowing that his wife's income wouldn't cover the family's expenses, Kevin worried what she would say when he told her about his Journey of Discovery. They had a mortgage and many other bills, not to mention their kids' college tuitions. How would she react if Kevin told her he was considering options outside the traditional career path, especially if some of those options meant the family budget might take a temporary hit?

Kevin's wife did indeed share many of his fears. However, she did not have the benefit of having experienced the same Journey of Discovery. While Kevin's paradigms shifted as he pictured the future he had always wanted and saw that the path he was currently on would not get him there, his wife could only see the obstacles and risks threatening her family. Kevin realized this challenge, and he got his wife and family involved in the experience. Doing so allowed them to take the Journey of Discovery together, so that they could use each other as sounding boards and discuss how they were feeling about what they were learning. After all, a change in Kevin's career would impact them all, and especially when going into business for himself.

Kevin's YOU 2.0®

For Kevin, creating his YOU 2.0® caused him to reflect on some thought-provoking questions, and as he started contemplating the dangers facing him and his family in the future, he realized that many of them were common concerns and obstacles experienced by other people like him embarking on a new and different career path.

Although one of his primary worries was that his hard-earned skills wouldn't be transferable to a new job, Kevin's biggest anxiety actually involved his age. At 50 years old, Kevin had been working in PR for decades, but he knew that many companies wanted to hire younger employees at lower salaries. If he were to leave his current job, how likely would it be that another company would hire a man nearing retirement age?

Once Kevin had taken time to address his concerns, he was prompted by his Entrepreneur's Source coach to talk and write about his desires for the future—he found that earning enough to pay for his children's education while still being able to build the wealth and equity that could support him and his wife after they retire was very important to him. They had always talked about traveling more once their work years were behind them, and Kevin wanted to make sure they could still live out those dreams. If he continued at his present job, this dream was becoming more and more unreachable.

Finally, Kevin documented his strengths. As an ad executive, he was creative as well as organized and deadline-oriented. He was great with clients and had developed a large network of friends and colleagues in both the business world and his community. Although Kevin worried that some of his skills would not transfer well into a new career, The Entrepreneur's Source Journey of Discovery offered tools that allowed him to see just how valuable those skills and traits could be in any industry.

By the end of his Journey of Discovery, Kevin was feeling much better about what he had to offer and which skills would help him on his new career path. He felt all of the expected fear and anxiety but worked through those feelings and decided not to make decisions based on emotion but rather on fact, and started down the road towards greater Income, Lifestyle, Wealth, and Equity.

John

Baby boomer, John, whom we met in previous chapters, is nearing retirement age. He is concerned that his Social Security and his pension are just not going to cut it. He and his wife want to travel and enjoy their retirement years, but John knows that, without his usual paycheck, the dreams of travel don't look too promising. Having heard from a friend about how The Entrepreneur's Source can help people work on their YOU 2.0®, he decides to meet with an Entrepreneur's Source coach and explore what options might exist for him after he retires from his current job.

During the first meeting, John's coach, David, asks John about his picture of the future. *"Well,"* John begins, *"my wife and I have spent our entire lives working and raising our kids. We have always said we want to travel more, and now might be our last chance to do it. I am not getting any younger, and I want to make sure that, after I retire, I will have enough money to keep some of my lifestyle, travel, and maybe save some money for the grandkids."*

Working on YOU 2.0® makes all of this doable, as David points out, but John is not as certain.

"I'm not looking for another full time job—that is why I am retiring—but I need something more than just my pension. At my age, what kind of options am I looking at?"

It's then that David asks John the following question: *"If we looked at your life a year from today, what has to have happened during that period, both personally and professionally, for you to be happy with your progress?"* Deciding the answer to that question is what working toward the next version of you, YOU 2.0®, is all about. And that is when coach David introduces the concept and the value of the Journey of Discovery, the process of education and exploration John will undergo before making any decisions.

"Once you're certain you have explored all of your options and have a better idea of where you want to end up in five years' time, we will look at some business models and learn whether they have the potential to get you where you want to go."

As the coaching sessions go on, John with the assistance of David clarifies what he wants more of in his life. He starts to create a vision of what his new life can look like after retirement. He starts to see all the possibilities that were not even a fleeting thought before. In time David introduces a few business models to John.

"But I don't know anything about these industries," John claims. *"I mean, I don't even like frozen yogurt! How can I operate a frozen yogurt franchise? None of these businesses are right for me."*

"Look, before you make any decisions," David counsels him, *"talk to some of their franchisees. See how they've made these businesses work for them. I'd be curious to hear what you learn about their motivations."*

Still not sure about all of this, John decides to give his coach the benefit of the doubt, and joined by his wife, he educates himself on each model, talks to the franchisees, and gets a better feeling for these businesses as vehicles rather than as an extension of the career he is about to leave.

Just as he is narrowing down his possibilities—honing in on the yogurt franchise, of all things—John's doubts start to re-emerge. The company he currently works for would like to keep John on as a consultant, and he is tempted to take the opportunity. However, after thinking it through, John realizes that the job with his old company is not as secure as he would like to believe. Besides, at a decreased salary level, and with the sporadic nature of consulting work, it simply would not give him the Income, Lifestyle, Wealth, and Equity he now knows he needs in order to live the future he is envisioning.

John asks David about when the training sessions for the yogurt franchise take place and, without even realizing it, moves beyond the decision-making phase. He is ready to seize the future he has always wanted.

Doug

After running across our YOU 2.0® online, recent college graduate Doug has a completely different set of challenges compared to John.

"With all of the loans I had to take out just to finish school," he explains, *"I'm already in debt, and I'm not even 28 years old. I majored in business so that I could land a great job after I graduated, but it has only been two years, and I've already had to change jobs three times. I cannot even propose to my girlfriend because I do not have any savings. How can I even think about being self-sufficient when I can barely make my monthly loan payments?"*

"*Well,*" his coach, Diana, explains, "*it sounds like we have met at the right time. It may be time for you to work on the next version of you. Are you ready for YOU 2.0®? If so, I will work with you under one condition. You need to promise to keep an open mind and make no decisions prematurely. If I find that you are not doing that, do I have your permission to point that out to you? I will have you explore some options other than the ones your college career counselor exposed you to.*"

"*I don't have any problems with exploring some different options, and I think I can be pretty open-minded about whatever you show me, but I am worried I might be too young to start thinking about self-sufficiency,*" said Doug. "*I mean, shouldn't I pay my dues in the corporate world first?*"

"*That's a common worry,*" Diana claims. "*But we aren't living in your parents' job market. Do you feel that college has not adequately prepared you to be financially independent and have a successful career? What worked for the previous generation is not going to work for you. Is trying to 'pay your dues' in the corporate world going to get you where you want to go? Many of our clients, young and old, have found that taking charge of their careers is the best way to get them where they want to go. They have figured out that they do not want to continue to work on somebody else's dream; they need to work on their own. The fact that you get to contemplate and learn about all your possibilities at this point in your life and career is truly a blessing. I know I have many clients who would have loved to have found the road to self-sufficiency at your age. Remember, I am not asking you to make any decisions right now. What I am asking of you is to keep an open mind and educate yourself about all your options."*

In the end, Doug concludes that Diana is right—what does he have to lose? He only has insights to gain—and decides to embark on the Journey of Discovery. It may go against everything he has been taught, but it turns out, that is just the direction he needs to follow.

Beth

"Look," corporate executive Beth begins her session with her coach, Sean, *"my current job just is not working for me anymore. I make a great salary, sure, but I see more of the airport than I do my house. I need something different, something that lets me keep my current income but allows me to have more free time and less travel."*

"A friend of mine went through your program and is doing great, so I thought I might give it a try. Just let me know how much I need to invest."

Listening to what Beth is hoping to get out of a new career path, Sean begins by assuring her that he does not charge for his time, and other than some books or educational programs he may recommend, the biggest investment right now will be her commitment to being open to learning new things. "This process is about exploration and education. It is just as much about figuring out what you want your future to look like as it is about finding the business that will work for you."

"But I already know what I want, and I've done all the research on the latest business models out there. I just need you to tell me what the sure-fire industries and investments are."

"There are no guarantees here," Sean explains. "Our Journey of Discovery is designed to help you explore your goals, needs, and expectations and to allow you to gain clarity about what you want the next version of you to look like, hence, YOU 2.0°, and then look at business models that can be used as vehicles to serve your life's purpose. Did you know that 95 percent of our clients end up in something they admittedly would have never looked at on their own or had previously dismissed? This statistic surprises many of our clients."

Sean piques Beth's interest and she engages him as her coach. Through working on her YOU 2.0°, by defining her Income, Lifestyle, Wealth and Equity expectations, she comes to realize that the solutions she needs are not in falling for the latest hot industry or job trend. Instead, she begins to really examine her current situation and her goals for the future, eventually coming to the conclusion that self-sufficiency is the only way to take control of her life and destiny.

As a single woman, she does not have a family to question her decision, although her friends and coworkers are stunned when Beth tells them that she is planning to leave her stable corporate job to pursue the path to self-sufficiency. What about her paycheck and her 401(k)? Has she seen the statistics on the rate of failure for small businesses?

Beth listens to all of these points and begins to doubt that this is the right path for her. Her concerns grow after seeing the business models her coach has presented; none of them seem even remotely connected to her area of expertise. How will her skills transfer into any of these industries? If she should embark on one of these business models and fail, how will she ever re-enter the corporate world at her current job level and salary?

"You have to look at the models as vehicles and not an extension of your current career," Sean advises her. *"You are not buying yourself a job; you are using this new business as a way of achieving the flexibility you want. I am sure you are not the only person to have ever had this concern; why don't you speak to a few more people who have taken the leap and learn what they have found to be the case. Remember, feeling nervous about embarking on something new is normal, but is making the change worth it, even if it means being temporarily uncomfortable, if you have more to gain than lose?"*

Beth does some soul searching and looks past the

corporate world, beyond the fads she thought she needed, and finds a path that will help her achieve her desired lifestyle, while still maintaining and increasing her income, wealth and equity.

Emily

When Emily was introduced to her coach, her biggest concern was providing for her two children.

"I have a stable job and a paycheck," she tells her coach. *"But I never have any time to spend with my kids. All my energy goes into my work, and I feel like I am missing watching them grow up. I am a single mom, and I just want something that will give me enough money to provide for my son and daughter without making me sacrifice my time with them."*

Emily's coach, Grace, tells her, *"Our mission is to help you achieve the income, lifestyle, wealth and equity you want."* Grace goes on to explain the Journey of Discovery. She tells her about working on her YOU 2.0®, defining her goals, and learning about different business models.

"Wait a minute," Emily stops Grace the moment she hears about the business models. *"Owning my own business? There's no way I could do that. It would be even more time consuming than my current job. I may have to deal with fewer conference calls and meetings, but running a business could tie me up with more administrative tasks."*

"And what if the business fails? I may have to put in a lot of hours right now, but at least I have a steady paycheck coming in."

"I can certainly understand your concerns about what it takes to run your own business. What if you were to find out that there are other people in similar situations to yours that have been able to achieve what you say you want? Would it make a difference? What if you were to find out that your knee-jerk reaction is in fact false evidence appearing real? I am not trying to sell you a business; the Journey of Discovery is a time-tested process that allows you to educate yourself about the possibilities that exist, so that you can create a better future for yourself and your family. My role as a coach is simply to ask questions and challenge you on limiting beliefs that may be holding you back from the life you say you want. There are a lot of misconceptions about the time it takes to run your own business. But as your coach, I represent your interest first and foremost. I deal with clients who have similar concerns to the ones you've raised all the time," Grace reassures Emily.

"I can understand your concern about leaving the security of a corporate paycheck. Are you ever concerned that it may go away? Are you ever concerned about layoffs or the possibility of your company merging or downsizing? Many of my clients are. They feel let down, and that is why I urge everybody to, at the very least, educate themselves about the possibilities that exist for you and your family, and then to do what is right and makes most sense for your situation," Grace explains.

After listening to Grace, Emily takes an honest look at her current career and decides to take the Journey of Discovery. Sure enough, she finds that all of her assumptions about the security of the corporate world have changed. She may have a steady paycheck at the moment, but that situation could change almost instantly. She realizes she is working to increase someone else's income, lifestyle, wealth, and equity, while never getting the opportunity to build those things for herself and her children.

Guided by her coach, Emily begins exploring options outside her comfort zone and starts to see that she owes it to her son and daughter to overcome the fear dragon and build a future for all of them—one where she doesn't have to give up attending her son's parent-teacher night or her daughter's recital just to make ends meet.

In these four examples, the clients coming to The Entrepreneur's Source have different backgrounds and motivations. Yet their Journey of Discovery ends with the same results: increased Income, Lifestyle, Wealth, and Equity.

CHAPTER 8: RESOURCES AND WORKSHEETS

Questions to Ponder

Where is your professional future headed?

Are you on track?

Will your current path take you where you want to go?

What would happen if you started spending all those hours doing something for yourself?

What would your life look like? What would you do if failure were not an option?

Do you tend to take the path of least resistance and avoid looking at yourself and take responsibility for your life and future?

Do you close yourself to possibilities just because you have never considered them before?

Are you afraid of change?

How would you describe your feelings about your present career?

What do you want more of in your life, personally and professionally?

What do you want less of in your life, personally and professionally?

Five years from now, if you stay on your current career path:

- How do you see your options?

- How do you see yourself achieving financial independence?

What are your biggest concerns about changing careers?

If you knew you couldn't fail, what career would you choose?

If we looked at your life a year from today, what has to have happened during that period, both personally and professionally, for you to be happy with your progress?

In your present job:

- Are you feeling under-appreciated?

- How about feeling left out of important decisions or stymied by bureaucratic flab?

- Are you in a dead-end job, waiting your turn for that pink slip?

- Do you ever feel you could do great things if you could run the show?

What do you worry about?

What makes you afraid?

What causes anxiety for you?

What keeps you away from making a change?

What makes you run the other way when someone brings it up?

Are you even aware of all the voices of fear and all of its disguises?

YOUR PRIMARY AIM

It's About Your Life

Your Primary Aim is your innermost driving force. It's the source of the vitality, the commitment, the vision you need in order to get the most out of your life and have a business that will serve your life's purpose. It's that which, more than anything else, gives you a sense of direction and purpose, motivates you to your highest levels of energy, and sustains you over the long haul.

The Elusive Primary Aim

The vast majority of people aren't in touch with their Primary Aim. It's there, within all of us, but most of us simply haven't identified it.

Is it really that important? Yes, it is.

Understanding your Primary Aim gives you the ability to actively shape your life rather than passively accept whatever joy and whatever pain happens to come your way.

Your core values, beliefs, and desires shape your Primary Aim. Most people don't understand their core values very well, and many have false impressions about them. It seems odd that so many people aren't very aware of their Primary Aim because we all have a built-in barometer to tell us when we are in touch with it, and if we are affecting it in negative or positive ways. The barometer is our feelings and our emotions. If we pay attention and are aware, our emotional barometer can lead us to our Primary Aim.

We just have to pay attention.

Primary Aim Is More Pragmatic Than You Think

Primary Aim is not a New Age trend or the latest self-help gimmick. We're talking about a fundamental part of you, the part that propels you through life joyfully.

Red Herrings in Your Search for Your Real Primary Aim

Money, status, power, competition, possessions, celebrity—none of these are the real driving forces in your life. They can be important in their own way, but in themselves aren't driving forces in your life. They can also be red herrings that distract you in the search to understand your Primary Aim. Your Primary Aim is something deeper, more fundamental, more you.

How Do You Determine Your Primary Aim?

There is a very introspective process that will help you achieve a clear understanding of your Primary Aim. Some people breeze through it easily. Others are challenged and go through bouts of confusion and self-appraisal before they understand what their Primary Aim is all about. Virtually everyone learns from it.

The end result is to create a force for guiding your life and the important elements within your life, including your future business.

It's All About You

Your Primary Aim is unique to you. It's about what you truly want for yourself. It's not about the obligations you have to others, and it's not about what others expect of you.

Think only about yourself and what you want your life to be like. That's difficult for many of us. We are accustomed to putting others first or taking responsibility for them. For the moment, let go of all these responsibilities and "shoulds." Indulge yourself and think only in terms of your own self-interest. Dream and fantasize. Reach for what you want.

Feel free to let your wishes soar without embarrassment, self-consciousness, or concern for the expectations of others.

Look for the "Fire"

It takes careful thought to discover your Primary Aim, the one that fits you uniquely, the one that provides a sense of direction and purpose, and the one you feel in your gut. It's easy to come up with something that "sounds good" and that "should be" a good Primary Aim, but doesn't really motivate you. It would be a mistake to navigate the process and the worksheets we will share with you to arrive at a Primary Aim that seems okay, but that in your heart-of-hearts just doesn't have the fire of your most heartfelt purpose in life.

Make an honest self-assessment, figure out what you really want from your life, condense it into a brief statement, and use it as a guiding light as you plan your future.

What Don't You Want?

Often it's easier to know what you don't want than what you do want. A good way to begin the search for your Primary Aim is to become very clear about all the things you know you don't want. Make a list. Don't stop writing until you've written down everything you can think of.

There is a basic premise at work here, which says that focusing on what you don't want creates more of the same. The things you know you don't want are probably things you think about frequently. You probably play them over and over again in your mind. The result is that you are mentally "rehearsing" them, practicing them, reinforcing them.

In sports and music, there is a technique called visualization. The athlete or musician mentally goes through the right motions in preparation for the actual event. It has been proven to be a powerful technique for improving performance, and the same technique works for improving any other aspect of your life.

But there is a dark side. If you are in the habit of fault-finding and focusing on what goes wrong, then your mind stays on the negative, and even though you wish for the positive, you are mentally rehearsing the negative. It's a tough habit to overcome. After all, if you are told not to think about a pink elephant, what's the first thing that pops into your mind? If you are repeatedly told, or tell yourself, to avoid something, what stays on your mind?

Why do we start your Primary Aim exploration by focusing on the negative? It's simply a way of discovering what you really do want. Once you have a clear picture of what you don't want, it can be a simple process of reversing the items to determine what you truly do want.

What Do You Want?

When do you feel most free? What is it that makes you feel most in touch with yourself? What gives you the greatest sense of fulfillment? Everyone has peak experiences. What are they for you? What do you want your life to stand for? What's really important to you? This is what your Primary Aim is all about.

Again, you start by making a list. Think about what you appreciate, what is important to you, the parts of your life you treasure, the ones that give you your deepest sense of satisfaction? If your list fills up with material things, dig deeper. Your Primary Aim isn't about "stuff." It's about being alive.

What Gets in Your Way?

Here's a prediction. As you make your do-want list, you'll think of some things you will be tempted to ignore because, "That's not realistic for me." Or "I don't have the ability to . . . ." Do not impose limitations on yourself! For the most part, limitations turn out to be more imaginary than real. And even completely unrealistic wishes, if they are heartfelt, give you valuable information about your core values.

Consider, for instance, David, a 63-year-old owner of a successful auto repair franchise in Ohio. David yearned to ride the space shuttle. It was a heartfelt, deep-seated desire of his, but impossible to achieve. He didn't add it to his do-want list, but did mention it in a conversation, and it turned out to be an important hint about his Primary Aim.

David discovered that being in outer space and looking back at the Earth had qualities that were important to him, and that he imagined would be intensely gratifying— qualities having to do with being in touch with great ideas and widespread importance. He learned, after some discussion, that he could attain that same feeling of gratification and fulfillment by doing public benefit work in highly visible positions with charitable organizations.

He even found a way to involve his business and the entire franchise network in contributing to this higher cause. His self-limiting perception of the impossibility of space travel had blinded him to a real source of gratification and the wide range of life experiences that could be truly satisfying to him.

The point? Don't ignore heartfelt desires simply because they seem impossible, undeserved, embarrassing, inappropriate, or not within your grasp. Dig within yourself for the source of the emotion behind the desire, and see where that leads you. More often than not, it will lead you to a new source of fulfillment.

Questions to Stimulate Thinking

About Your Primary Aim - Question yourself, and then question your answers.

The following list of questions can stimulate your thinking and put you in the right frame of mind for working on your Primary Aim. Take time to think about your answers. There are, of course, no right or wrong answers, just answers that are true for you. Some of the questions are easy some are difficult; and some may cause you to rethink your most basic values and attitudes. Most importantly, be honest with yourself.

Don't force yourself to answer every question. Pick the ones that catch your eye and provoke strong emotions in you. As you go through the Discovery Process, refer back to these initial thoughts to remind you of the things that make you feel truly passionate and inspired about life.

Questions to stimulate your thinking about your Primary Aim

- What do you want your life to look and feel like?

- What do you value most? What's important to you?

- What matters most at this point in your life?

- What would you like to be able to say about your life after it's too late to do anything about it?

- Many years from now, at your funeral, what do you hope will be said about you in your eulogy?

- How do you want your life to feel on a day-to-day basis?

- What would you like people's perceptions of you to be?

- What are your daydreams about?

- When you were young, what did you want to be when you grew up?

- Do you ever find yourself wishing you were different? What do you wish? Why aren't you that way? What gets in your way?

- Of all the things you have done in your life, what has given you the most satisfaction or pleasure?

- Of all the things you have done in your life, what has given you the least satisfaction or pleasure?

- If you no longer had to work, how would you spend your time? And with whom?

- What is missing from your life? When you find yourself wishing for something, what is it?

- What motivates you to perform above and beyond the call of duty?

  - What are your greatest strengths?

  - What are your greatest weaknesses?

  - What do you want to achieve, but you find it impossible to do? What barriers make it impossible? Think again, are those barriers really insurmountable?

Your Primary Aim Discovery Process

Your Primary Aim is a matter of discovery, not invention. You don't create your Primary Aim. It already exists within you. The Primary Aim Process is a way of discovering what is already there.

For most people, the process involves new ways of looking at themselves and their lives. It asks that you question your assumptions about life and your own core values. It requires that you use your feelings—your internal barometer—to guide you. It is a very personal experience, a process that gets you in touch with what is truly and fundamentally important to you.

This is where a Coach can be of great value to you. A Coach is like a tour guide, helping you through this self-discovery process. A Coach doesn't provide answers for you; he or she asks questions to facilitate the process of self-discovery. Can you take this Journey on your own? Absolutely...but the benefits of having a tour guide while going through uncharted territory are significant.

You start the Primary Aim Process by quickly making lists of what you want and do not want in your life. Then you apply your thoughts and your feelings to the lists, narrowing them down to the most important do-wants and don't-wants. Next, you identify what gets in the way of your Primary Aim, and finally, you condense your findings into a brief statement of the essence of your Primary Aim. The process can be intense at times, but it's always rewarding. It's one of the most valuable things you will ever do for yourself.

It's a five-step process:

1. **What you don't want.** Make a long list of what you don't want in your life. Don't think too much about each item. When your list is complete, go back over it. This time think carefully about each item and be aware of the feelings it stirs. Circle the items that trigger the strongest negative emotions, the things you most want to not be part of your life. Don't circle more than a few items; focus on the most important ones.

Below list everything that causes you anger, stress, frustration, fear, hatred, embarrassment, or displeasure. Include whatever it is that you do not want in your life. Don't think too much about it, just write as many as you can think of and as freely as you can. You can use a notebook or pad if you prefer.

_____

_____

_____

_____

_____

_____

_____

_____

Now go back over your list, thinking carefully about each item. Notice your feelings, the sense of importance you give to each one. Select the few items, no more that 5 or 6, that you want the least in your life. Place an asterisk after each item you select to identify them as the least desirable items.

2. **What you do want.** Quickly make another long list of what you do want in your life. Stay away from material things and money—they have little or nothing to do with your Primary Aim. As before, go back over the list and circle the items you most want

to be part of your life. This time, circle the items that have the strongest attraction, the strongest positive feelings. Don't circle more than a few items—one, two, a half-dozen at most.

Now list below everything that you do want in your life. Look at your deepest desires. Focus on what makes you feel happy, fulfilled, satisfied, energized, motivated, inspired, and purposeful. Avoid the superficial and the material, focusing on the deeply satisfying, profoundly rewarding life experiences. Again, don't think too much about it, just write as many as you can and use a pad if necessary.

_____

_____

_____

_____

_____

_____

_____

_____

Also as before, go back over your list, thinking carefully about each item. Again, notice your feelings, the sense of importance you assign to each one. Select the few items, no more that 5 or 6, that are the things you want most in your life and rank them from the most important to the least important. Indicate the most important items with asterisks. Then place a number in front of each selected item to indicate its priority.

3. **Prioritizing and breaking barriers.** Copy the circled items from your do-want list onto a new list. Think about each item and rank them in order of importance. Then for each one, think about what it is that gets in the way of achieving it. What blocks you from having your do-wants? Finally—and this is important—identify your self-imposed limitations. What barriers do you put in your way that limit beliefs about yourself and endorse counterproductive habits?

Use the worksheet below to record the things you want the most of in your life—your priorities and the barriers that may be blocking you from achieving them and what can solve the blockage. Write the things you want in order of importance. Think carefully about each of them, and write down what, if anything, is keeping you from them. Always give special thought to self-imposed limitations.

Important things you want in life:	Barriers and Limitations:	Barrier-Breakers/ Solutions:

4. **Write your eulogy.** Think of that far-off day when you are gone and all the people who are most important to you are assembled at your memorial ceremony. You get to write your own eulogy. What do you want it to say? What do you want to be remembered for? Think through your life–remember what makes you proud.

5. **Write your Primary Aim.** In the fewest possible words, write a statement of the essence of your Primary Aim. Try for a phrase or a single sentence

that describes what you want your life to be like in order for it to express what's most important to you. Remember, the acid test for your Primary Aim statement is your internal barometer. When you read Your Primary Aim, you should feel energized, enthusiastic, committed, a sense of, "Yes! This is me!" If not, you haven't gotten it. Keep trying.

Bringing Your Primary Aim to Life

Your Personal Objectives Should Be Consistent with Your Primary Aim.

Personal objectives are the specific, tangible goals you want to accomplish, and you should develop a way to track the extent to which a business will be supporting the life you desire. Your business should serve your life, not the other way around. You'll know that you've got your priorities aligned with your Primary Aim when you meet your stated personal objectives, one by one, over time.

For example, how many vacation days would you like to spend with your family? How many golf days per month? Is there a professional accreditation you would like to acquire? A vacation home? Time to enjoy your hobbies? When your business is serving your life, there is room for the people, activities and interests that make your life enjoyable and satisfying. Where do you start? By getting clear about what you want, writing it down, and making it happen.

Personal objectives are goals that are tangible and measurable. They can be material in nature. They can be financial benchmarks. Or they can be quality-of-life indicators (volunteering in your child's classroom once a month, for instance). The pattern of your personal objectives shapes the pattern of your life.

Choose your personal objectives carefully and they'll keep you in harmony with your Primary Aim.

PERSONAL OBJECTIVES WORKSHEET

Component	In 6 Months	In 12 Months	In 5 Years	In 10 Years+
Income:				
Annual Income				
Investment Income				
Other Income				
Lifestyle:				
Family and Relationships				
Hobbies and Pastimes				
Travel and Leisure				
Time to volunteer				
Education and Personal Development				
Major Purchases				
Other:				
Wealth:				
Investments				
Retirement				
Professional Growth				
Other:				
Equity:				
Property:				
Other:				
Other:				
Other:				

(Endnotes)

1. http://beforeitsnews.com/alternative/2012/10/77-per-cent-of-all-americans-live-paycheck-to-paycheck-at-least-part-of-the-time-2477022.htmland http://www.globalresearch.ca/37-facts-about-how-cruel-this-econ-omy-has-been-to-millions-of-desperate-american-fami-lies/5309938

2. William R. Mattox, Jr., "The Parent Trap," Policy Re-view, no. 55, Winter, 1991, p. 6.

3. http://edition.cnn.com/2001/CAREER/trends/08/30/ilo.study/

4. Monthly Labor Review • September 2010

80504630R00073

Made in the USA
San Bernardino, CA
28 June 2018